An Extraordinary Life

A Māori woman's journey to find success while overcoming her own tortured past

Toni Te Kowhai

First published by Ultimate World Publishing 2024
Copyright © 2024 Toni Te Kowhai

ISBN

Paperback: 978-1-923123-52-6
Ebook: 978-1-923123-53-3

Toni Te Kowhai has asserted her rights under the Copyright, Designs and Patents Act 1988 to be identified as the author of this work. The information in this book is based on the author's experiences and opinions. The publisher specifically disclaims responsibility for any adverse consequences which may result from use of the information contained herein. Permission to use information has been sought by the author. Any breaches will be rectified in further editions of the book.

All rights reserved. No part of this publication may be reproduced, stored in or introduced into a retrieval system, or transmitted in any form, or by any means (electronic, mechanical, photocopying, recording or otherwise) without the prior written permission of the author. Any person who does any unauthorised act in relation to this publication may be liable to criminal prosecution and civil claims for damages. Enquiries should be made through the publisher.

DISCLAIMER

The opinions expressed in this book are those of the author. They do not purport to reflect the opinions or views held by Corrective Services or its members. The designations employed in this book and presentations of material therein do not imply the expression or views of any legal entity referred to but includes the authors carefully considered and challenging views and stories on such topics about domestic violence, sexual assault, deportation, young offenders and are given immediacy and authority by being entirely written in the author's own words. She has not forgotten her cultural roots nor her pride in them.

Cover design: Ultimate World Publishing
Layout and typesetting: Ultimate World Publishing
Editor: James Salmon

Ultimate World Publishing
Diamond Creek,
Victoria Australia 3089
www.writeabook.com.au

In Gratitude

My father told me when I was growing up "I could be anything I wanted to be" .... if only I knew what that was...? How does a young Māori girl cross the Tasman Sea, leaving behind her family, friends, her whole support network to follow her dreams and start fresh?

I was born from a rich traditional cultural Māori heritage. Proud to be Māori, the drive to 'stand on my own two feet' is strong.

I pursued grace with the same commitment, perseverance and determination.

I love you Dad - you are forgiven and will never be forgotten.

Testimonial

I am pleased to give a testimonial about my 6 year working relationship with Toni Te Kowhai at the Parklea Correctional centre, Sydney Australia.

My name is Mark Peteru // I have a total of 32 years operational experience with NSW corrections.

My current work role is supervisor for Inmate classification and placement.

Toni was my direct supervisor and manager from when I commenced employment at Parklea in 2016, and from the outset, to prepare me for the role, Toni conducted one-on-one orientation, workshops, and follow-up instruction that equipped me with the necessary and updated knowledge, as well as the tools to be effective and efficient in my duties and responsibilities.

Within a year, Toni enabled my enrolment on the Certificate IV Trainer and Assessors course// as well as enrolment in the State-run "Classification and Placement training" at the Corrective Services Brush Farm Academy. Toni made ongoing requests to management // to place me and my fellow supervisors on relevant courses for further professional development.

I was privileged and grateful to accompany Toni to two consecutive Annual Corrective Services Classification and Placement Conferences, knowing that she pushed for management approval so I could attend these high-level meetings. I observed at these conferences that Toni was able to seamlessly participate and contribute well during the sessions that were attended by the Director of Inmate classification, regional managers, and assorted specialists from the private-run and State-run sectors.

Toni has a compassionate, direct, firm, and fair approach to managing staff. Because she possesses such a strong work ethic, Toni's expectation is that her staff follow suit in maintaining the highest standard and performance.

As a result of the leadership and guidance of Toni Te Kowhai at Parklea, and might I add especially through the COVID restrictions, the Parklea inmate classification and placement team are acknowledged throughout the centre as professional, competent, and available to provide support to staff and inmates when and where required.

A wonderful legacy to reflect on.

Thank you

Contents

In Gratitude — iii
Testimonial — v
About The Author — ix
Foreword — 1
1. Childhood Turmoil and Growth — 3
2. What's Gang Rape? — 21
3. A New Beginning in Australia — 27
4. Trying to Fit — 37
5. That's Called Racism — 41
6. A Can-Do Attitude — 45
7. Cavalry Has Arrived — 51
8. Fostering a Culture of Respect — 55
9. He's My Soulmate — 63
10. Like a Boss — 75
11. Next Generation Leaders — 79
12. Searching for Grace — 85
Acknowledgements — 93
References — 95

About The Author

Toni Te Kowhai's journey is a testament to resilience and unwavering determination. Arriving in Australia in 1981 with a young son, she faced the challenges of divorce at a tender age. It was only in 1993 that she officially became a naturalised Australian. Her quest for personal growth began when she enrolled in a TAFE course designed for women seeking to re-enter the workforce.

As a mature-age student, she transitioned to university after successfully completing a bridging course, initially pursuing IT before finding her true calling. In 2000, she graduated with a Bachelor's Degree in Business Human Resource Management/Industrial Relations (HRM/IR), solidifying her passion for HRM.

Toni's career journey commenced with various casual jobs before an encounter with a friend from her church congregation led her to a remarkable role as a detention officer at the Villawood Immigration Detention Centre (VIDC). Her commitment to service at VIDC continued for four years before love led her to corrections, a field her partner was familiar with.

Joining the Department of Corrections as a Committee Officer for the Serious Offenders Review Council (SORC), Toni embraced opportunities for secondments in challenging roles, including Emu Plains and Parramatta Gaols, gaining valuable experience in classification and placement.

Over time, her role evolved, guiding her towards admin support for the Manager of Classification and Placement Indigenous Programs. Destiny intervened when she was approached by the first Māori Superintendent at Long Bay Gaol to become the Secretary of the Pacific Island Offender Program Steering Committee, fostering her understanding of Indigenous cultures in the correctional system.

Headhunted by Global Excellence and Outsourcing (GEO), Toni played a pivotal role in managing Parklea Correctional Centre as the Case Management Coordinator. Her dedication over 12 and a half years left an indelible mark on this maximum-security facility, overseeing a team of 10 staff. Beyond her professional commitments, Toni actively engaged with her community, participating in initiatives like the Sydney Marae Fundraising Appeal and representing the Māori community leaders and elders.

In 2022, Toni retired as a Senior Classification & Placement Officer for another private company MTC Broadspectrum, having made an enduring impact on the NSW correctional system. Her legacy is not only marked by her team's distinction but by her unwavering commitment to integrity, professionalism, and empowering leadership. Toni's story serves as an inspiration to all who encounter her remarkable journey of growth, resilience, and dedication.

About The Author

"Our deepest fear is not that we are inadequate, our deepest fear is that we are powerful beyond all measure. It is our light, not our darkness that most frightens us. We ask ourselves, 'Who am I to be brilliant, gorgeous, talented, fabulous?' Actually, who are you not to be? You are a child of GOD. Your playing small does not serve the world. There is nothing enlightened about shrinking so other people do not feel insecure around you. We were born to make manifest the Glory of God that is within us. It's not just in some of us; it's in everyone. And, as we let our own light shine, we unconsciously give other people permission to do the same. As we are liberated from our own fear, our presence automatically liberates others." (Marianne Williamson)

Foreword

HE PEPEHA	This is so you may know me
KO NGONGOTAHA TE MAUNGA	Mount Ngongotaha is my mountain
KO TE UTUHINA TE AWA	Utuhina is my stream
KO TE ARAWA TE WAKA	Te Arawa is my canoe
KO TE ARAWA TE IWI	Te Arawa are my people
KO NGATI WHAKAUE ME TUHOURANGI I TE HAPU TE RORO OTE RANGI ME	Ngati Whakaue and Tuhourangi are my ancestors and I belong to Te Roro ote Rangi
KO TONI TE KOWHAI TAKU INGOA	My name is Toni Te Kowhai
KO AU TE TAMAHINE A BARRYMORE WHAREKIRI TE KOWHAI RAUA KO HOANA HURIHANGANUI	My parents My father is Barry Te Kowhai and my mother is Joanne Hurihanganui
TI HEI MĀORI ORA	This is my life and these are my lifelines

An Extraordinary Life

This logo symbolises back-to-back support, protection and knowledge within the confines of our cultural heritage, traditions and customs. The back-to-back koru symbols represent the potential within us all and as well as being an individual thing, this is also a collective, community thing. United we have strength and energies have a continuous flow.
Dr B Pittman (2013) dec.

Childhood Turmoil and Growth

I have vivid memories of being eight years old. In my childhood, I was the middle child among five siblings, with a two-year age gap separating each of us. I had two elder sisters, the oldest of whom was raised by our grandparents. In addition, there was a younger brother and a little sister, all under the care of our parents, who were far too young for such a large family.

Our family home was conveniently situated just across the road from our primary school. On our way to school, we would often see the milkman delivering small glass bottles of milk. During our little lunch break, our teacher ensured that each student in our class received a bottle of milk along with a piece of fruit. Not far from our primary school, there was a park where we spent our warm summer afternoons, playing and enjoying ourselves.

An Extraordinary Life

The weekends held a special place in my memory due to the parties that would unfold on Scotts Avenue at night. I could often hear the sounds of guitars strumming and people singing, their voices echoing throughout the neighbourhood. I would lie in bed and hum along when I recognised the songs. However, some nights, especially late ones, I would overhear heated arguments in the hallway outside my bedroom door, fuelled by alcohol.

My dad was a violent alcoholic, and I would frequently hear my mum struggling as she tried to stifle her tears, fearing that any noise would wake me. I vividly remember the sound of my dad's fists striking her, the harsh impact echoing through the walls as she stumbled into them. It was a terrible noise that haunted me. I would bite my lip and resist the urge to get out of bed because the one time I did, I witnessed my dad hurting her, and it left a lasting scar on my young heart. I was too terrified to cry out loud and never left my bed again when their fights erupted in the hallway.

One fateful night, as I lay in bed, it seemed as if my world had descended into chaos. Instead of the delightful music that usually filled the air, the night was filled with shouting, fights, breaking furniture, and the sounds of cars speeding away. It wasn't until I grew older that I realised alcohol could escalate anger to such extreme levels.

My best friend, who also happened to be my cousin, informed me that it was her family that took in all the children wandering the streets in the middle of the night, wrapped in blankets, desperately seeking safety. One night, my elder sister quietly shook me awake and whispered in my ear to go to Aunty's house. Uncle would sit on his patio, waiting for the little ones to arrive, ushering us into their children's bedrooms, urging them to make room for us. It was there that we found warmth and safety.

Childhood Turmoil and Growth

I held a special place in my dad's heart because we would always have breakfast together, and he would bid me farewell each morning before heading off to work. But one Sunday morning, when I got out of bed early, my mum informed me that he had left without saying goodbye and wasn't coming back. For many years, I blamed myself for his departure. Seeing my mum's tear-streaked face and blackened eyes, I was too young to offer any help, but not too young to carry the weight of guilt.

In our Scotts Avenue neighbourhood, large families were common, and at one point, I could recite the surnames of every family residing in those homes. As the years passed, my mum raised us on her own. It was far from easy; she had to manage all the bills herself, a responsibility that had previously been my dad's as the primary breadwinner. We lacked running hot water, relying on an old copper that required a fire to boil water. We would take turns to have a bath while the water was still warm, leaving us with rosy cheeks and wrinkled toes.

We changed schools multiple times, and during one of those periods, we lived with our grandparents. Although my granddad worked as a painter at the local hospital, my grandmother had to take on two jobs to feed our ever-growing family. Eventually, my brother and I were sent to live with Dad and his girlfriend after a custody battle. For a while, my elder sister attempted to live with us, but she soon returned to Mum to help care for our youngest sister since Mum was now working.

Dad and his girlfriend came back to our hometown to live when my brother and I were approaching our teenage years. Over the years, my dad continued to be violent and abusive, sometimes even in our presence. They say children learn by example, so it was no surprise when my brother began to mimic his behaviour and hurt me when they were not around.

An Extraordinary Life

Though I was two years older, he was taller and stronger, making it difficult for me to defend myself. I would attempt to lock him out of my room after school, but he was determined, and I often ended up fleeing down the road, hiding in the bushes to complete my homework in safety until everyone returned from work. I withdrew from everyone, and Dad would dismiss it, labelling me as "the deep one," but my sensitivity was more of a defense mechanism.

We eventually moved in with Dad's mum to help care for her as her health declined. My nan could be a bit grumpy, but we got along well. Living with her had its advantages, as her house was just a stone's throw away from the city centre. I was now in middle school, and I enjoyed taking the bus to school with friends who lived near my grandparents. We had spent many school holidays together around Lake Rotorua making boats out of corrugated iron and would melt tar on a small open fire at the lakes edge to seal the holes and nail it all together with a prow made of wood. I would catch freshwater (koura) crayfish with my bare hands and boil them on the open fire in a tin – it made for good eating. On hot summer nights we would attach old car tyres and set it alight – the koura would walk right up onto the shores of the lake for us to gather up and cook on the fire and share with friends.

Every Saturday, I would visit the local movie theatre to watch a Kung Fu movie, and it was during one of those trips that I met a boy who simply wanted to kiss me. On our first official date, he waited outside our house while I finished up the breakfast dishes and when I joined him he held my hand and we walked to the movie theatre.

He became my first boyfriend, and we spent nights talking on the phone, getting to know each other when Dad wasn't home or when he was babysitting his little sister. As I grew older and tried to find my identity, I began doing typical teenage things to test my boundaries. One such instance was when I snuck out of the house through my bedroom window to attend a dance at a community centre and narrowly avoided getting caught while trying to sneak back in.

But not all my teenage experiences were so great. One weeknight, my teacher organised a barbecue at her house, and all my classmates were invited. Dad had no objections, so I was allowed to go. It was a pleasant evening, and I held my teacher in high regard because I learned a lot from her, and she considered me a good student. However, when it was time to leave her house, another teacher, with an air of inconvenience, informed me that he wasn't sure if he could make it to the petrol station since I lived so far away. Embarrassed, I quickly asked one of my friends if I could stay over at her place just for the night. She agreed, but because it was late, I debated whether to call home. I didn't want Dad to get out of bed and drive at night, especially if he had been drinking. The thought of him confronting me in front of everyone or, worse, speaking to my teacher filled me with shame and embarrassment.

When I returned home the next day, Dad was not at home. I explained what had happened to his girlfriend, but all she said was, "wait until your father gets home".

When Dad finally arrived, I had just stepped out of the bath with a towel wrapped around my head. I walked into the kitchen, intending to tell him what had transpired, but he struck me so hard across the face that my towel flew across the room. I had made a mistake, and now I was paying for it. I remember sobbing and apologising, but it seemed as though nothing I said mattered to him. He didn't believe me anyway.

My body was undergoing changes, and I was growing up, but it seemed that my own father no longer held any affection for me. Perhaps he thought I was no longer his little girl. After he hit me, I turned and went to my room, locking the door behind me. Having endured countless beatings from my brother over the years, my emotions were raw, and I realised this would not be the last time. So, I changed into different clothes, climbed out of the window, and walked away without looking back.

My mum lived twelve kilometres out of town, and I walked the entire way in the dark and rain. When I arrived, there were no lights on, so I assumed she was watching TV and entered the unlocked front door. Maybe it was the cold or my fatigue, but when I explained what had happened to her, I blurted out my greatest fear—that it was my fault and that he wouldn't stop hitting me now. I couldn't stay with him, and I pleaded with her to let me stay.

My mum immediately called Dad and relayed what I had said, informing him that I was going to stay with her until he had calmed down.

As I grew older and gained a deeper understanding, my mum, my little sister, and I would reminisce about our upbringing. Though we laughed awkwardly about the reasons behind our quirks and behaviours, we had been labelled as survivors of a dysfunctional family. In hindsight, the adage "What doesn't kill you, makes you stronger," attributed to 19th-century German philosopher Friedrich Nietzsche, seemed to fit our story perfectly. Thanks to Dad, *we had become resilient.*

I remember going to the movies with my niece to watch the movie "Once Were Warriors" based on a novel written by a NZ author Alan Duff in 1990 to portray the grim and shameful reality of the urban Māori, where alcoholism, poverty and DV threatened to define our culture (SBS NITV). Our communities were in real trouble, with police being called to a family violence incident every four minutes in 2017. Indeed NZ Parliament passed two major pieces of legislation – the Domestic Violence Act 1995 was repealed and replaced with the Family Violence Act in 2018. This new act provided improved protection for children and victims. There is a song in recent times that includes lyrics that highlight the need to not turn a blind eye to what's happening with regards to domestic violence. The song is sung by Stevie Wonder and BabyFace, and is called How Long.

"Grace is unfair, which is one of the hardest things about it. It is unreasonable to expect anyone to forgive the terrible things we or others do just because one apologises years later, unfair to ask the whanau (family) to overlook the many offences our teenage sons, our fathers, our sisters, our whanau has committed.

Grace, however, is not about fairness. What is true of families is also true of races, tribes and nations. Grace is powerful enough to break the chains that enslave generations. Grace alone melts ungrace." (P Yancey, 2002)

(A) My Youngest Brother

Upon my return from my elder sister's funeral, I couldn't help but wonder if my youngest brother would rise to face the greatest challenge of his life and leave an indelible mark on our family bonds.

Let me begin by mentioning that my aunt, the last surviving sibling of my father's generation, made it clear after our father's funeral that she wanted me to inform my stepmother and brother that they needed to vacate my grandparents' house shortly after his burial. This request weighed heavily on my conscience, as it meant rendering my young brother homeless in a time of grieving. Aunty had her reasons, though, and they were not entirely unjustified. It had been an open secret that my younger brother had been involved in selling drugs, hosted noisy parties, engaged in loud arguments with his girlfriend, and there were even allegations of burglary, among other issues. However, the paramount concern was the sorry state of disrepair our grandparents' home had fallen into.

Regrettably, Aunty decided to bypass any form of communication or consultation with us, the family members who held deep cultural ties and roots, about the occupancy of our grandparents' family home. Instead, she allowed her youngest son and his family to move in.

It makes me ponder whether I may be mistaken, but it's worth reflecting on how things are traditionally handled in our culture, which places immense importance on preserving our heritage for future generations. It's a unique argument, revolving around male lineage and succession planning, as well as safeguarding the legacy left by my grandfather to perpetuate our family name across generations. What saddens me deeply is the discovery of past decisions concerning Māori land made through the Māori Land Court without our knowledge or consultation.

There remains no one to contest the fact that her youngest son does not bear my grandparents' surname, yet he has secured the right to reside there for the duration of his life.

Upon our return from New Zealand, I forwarded my research findings to my youngest brother, who was born from my parents' union, in preparation for an application to challenge the validity of past decisions. The research methodology I employed mirrored the one I used during my time as a university student. I have full confidence that my brother, a capable individual in his own right who previously worked as a teacher and now serves as the Director of his own training company, will grasp the significance of the research.

The key to our endeavour lies in meticulous preparation of the facts. Given that this is a civil case, the process for presenting evidence in support of our claim differs from that in a criminal case. We do not require legal representation but can represent ourselves as we bring this claim before the court.

(B) The Remarkable Journey of My Aunt: A Pioneer in Restorative Justice

My aunt holds a special place in my heart, commanding my deepest respect as a true trailblazer. Several years ago, I had the privilege of listening to her share her remarkable story about Restorative Justice (RJ). At the time, I was working in the correctional services industry, and her narrative deeply resonated with me. I was attending an RJ conference as a surprise, driven by my aspiration to incorporate this transformative approach into a program we were developing for long-term inmates. RJ, at its core, revolves around the powerful idea of bringing victims and offenders together (Hudson, 2003).

To provide some context, my aunt's impressive resume includes the establishment of three social services agencies, certification as a clinical supervisor, and the esteemed honour of receiving a Queen's Honour Medal in 2006 for her community work. She dedicated a decade of her life to this field before retiring as a director.

My aunt's choice to work in family violence stemmed from an urgent need to respond to the escalating number of court referrals due to the harm inflicted on our women and children. She recognized that Māori men, perpetuating a cycle of abusive power, domination, and extreme violence within their families, needed to be held wholly accountable. Their harmful behaviours often stemmed from generational patterns that were far from positive.

Their approach involved direct engagement to convey crucial lessons, beyond the immediate consequences of continued violence—namely, the potential removal of their children and the deterioration of their relationships. A pivotal aspect was demonstrating to these men the profound impact of their violence on their children and highlighting the availability of help and the possibility of change. RJ, with its emphasis on addressing, restoring, and enhancing people's capacity to change, provided the framework for their efforts.

It's important to note that the RJ focus was just one facet of their comprehensive mission: supporting the family. Violence against women and children was seen as a grave violation of our Māori cultural values, centred on concepts of righteousness, integrity, and compassion. This approach proved highly effective in fostering change (The Rotorua Second Chance Community – Managed Restorative Justice Programme: An Evaluation).

During our conversations about my work in corrections and community diversion programs, I greatly valued my aunt's advice. The challenges were complex, and I believed that genuine rehabilitation within a prison environment, especially in a foreign country like Australia, presented even greater barriers.

Following my mother's passing, I expressed my gratitude to my aunt for attending her funeral upon my return to Sydney. Her response, conveyed through letters, revealed a poignant piece of our family history. In the early stages of my parents' marriage, they had all resided together in our grandparents' home, until they found a place to start their own families. This revelation, although I might have been just a baby at the time, added depth to my understanding. Recent Facebook photographs depicted our mother watching my two eldest sisters and our cousin (my aunt's daughter) playing in the sun, with our grandparents' house with the Papaiouru marae in the background.

In her letters from 2008, I sensed a genuine desire on my aunt's part to help our family, particularly our father, her younger brother, during an earlier period. It seemed that she had undertaken a profound journey of education and empowerment to assist other families in our community facing similar challenges. The societal and political ramifications of family violence have been undeniable, with extensive campaigns spanning several years aimed at teaching young boys to respect females and reject domestic violence. This initiative was complemented by the provision of crucial support agencies, offering online information and counselling referrals. Notably, this effort aimed to combat the leading cause of homelessness for women and children.

In conclusion, my aunt's inspiring journey in the realm of Restorative Justice stands as a testament to her unwavering commitment to our community, family, and the values we hold dear. Her transformative work continues to leave an indelible mark on those who have had the privilege of hearing her story and benefiting from her wisdom and dedication.

(C) Advocacy

Another such experience whilst I was a student at university which helped to shape my future direction came when I entered myself into the Inter-Varsity Advocacy Challenge, a process I found interesting and appealed to my competitive nature. This challenge was all about preparation. I read through so many books, some of which I had bought in my very first year of university about Human Resource Management.

We were a team of three and would be going up against students a year above us. Our opposition would be arguing the case for an Appeal, for an unfair dismissal case that was won earlier. The employee wanted to appeal the findings because she didn't think the compensation that she had won was enough. I was to prepare the closing argument and based on my findings, we would leave it to the Commissioner of Workplace Relations to decide who would win the challenge.

Our opening arguments were solid and based on the facts of the case. There were no witnesses to question, so we would rehash the facts of the case and we had to be convincing in our delivery to change the narrative. By sifting through the information and looking at it from a different perspective that may not have been considered at the time of the original hearing, we would argue whether the remedy was fair and equitable.

My other teammates were strong and determined and we had prepared meticulously with several meetings beforehand by reading out loud the original facts and began to pre-suppose what the other team would argue, thereby ensuring that we were on the same page from the outset. As we got to know each other, our roles became quite evident as we found our strengths through our own personal convictions.

Our argument came down to a management strategy about performance. This employee had received three warnings. The first – a verbal warning from her immediate supervisor – would communicate why her performance was found to be wanting and was either shown how to do the task more effectively (re-trained) or given advice to remind her what needed to be done, for the supervisor to gain compliance.

The time between the warnings is important for both parties. In these circumstances, the employee is given the opportunity to rectify her behaviour or undertake her duties more diligently by understanding exactly what she/he has done wrong. The supervisor could retrain and assess her work again to see if she had been successful. Unfortunately, this was not the case – time and again the employee did not demonstrate compliance, until they reached an impasse, and all three warnings were given. The supervisor, feeling he had no other recourse, dismissed her and she would have to look for another job.

It came as an absolute pleasure when the Commissioner of Workplace Relations handed down his decision – we had been successful in our pursuit and taken out the Inter-Varsity Advocacy Challenge. Though we celebrated each other's success, when my teammates and I spoke about what we considered the turning point, they gave me some real 'down to earth' feedback. Like a dog with a bone, I continued to concentrate on the original decision, compounding it with argument upon argument to change the narrative summary.

Indeed, we proved that with real teamwork, the employee won fair and equitable compensation the first time around, and the appeal for more was subsequently quashed. Truth be known, when one chooses to fight for justice, it's always better to argue when one knows all the facts of the matter, if one wants to be successful.

(D) Keeping the Faith

My grandfather was born on Mokoia Island on May 25, 1905, to Hiriwera Timihou Te Kowhai and Maraea Katoro Hapimana, both of Ngati Te Roro ote Rangi/Ngati Whakaue descent. He received his education in Rotorua and later attended Te Aute College in Hawke's Bay. There's a short story about my grandparents in a booklet called the Ohinemutu Informer, written by my father. It recounts how, after the war, my grandmother, fondly called Nan Flo, served as the cook at the

Childhood Turmoil and Growth

local hospital. At the end of her shifts, she would gather all the leftovers and prepare nutritious soups, bringing them home in plastic containers. My grandfather, Koro, would then distribute these soups throughout our community during the challenging depression years when jobs and food were scarce. Together with his brother, they would venture out on their little boat, moored next to the lake, to gather delicacies to include in the baskets. My Nan was resourceful too; she crafted clothing from scrap materials, knitted, and sewed, always ready to share and give.

In 1965, my Koro had the honor of becoming the first Maori and the last Mace Bearer for Rotorua at the opening of the monthly council meeting (as pictured above). Reading this story of my grandparents' kindness fills me with immense pride and respect (Ohinemutu Informer, Oct 2007, Issue 91, Publisher: Mahi Atua Cultural Trust, Est. 1989).

With unwavering faith, I continued to work during the pandemic. However, I was confined to my office, providing support to my team members who were custodial supervisors working within the prison. Many of our colleagues who were involved in hospital escorts had fallen ill to COVID, resulting in a significant reduction in our workforce.

During the second lockdown for COVID-19, a Maori friend and colleague I worked with at Parklea Correctional Centre called Operations to inform them that her son had contracted the virus at work. Consequently, she wouldn't be able to come to work as her entire family had tested positive for COVID, except for her youngest daughter. In a commendable effort to protect her youngest daughter, my friend isolated her within their bedroom, complete with an ensuite bathroom. This arrangement was made while she battled her own symptoms.

The prison staff rallied together to assemble a care package for them, filled with essential supplies and food. We delivered it to her doorstep, ensuring that transmission risks were minimised. I can still picture the moment when the door opened and the package was brought inside. For two long weeks, my friend and her family were in quarantine. Once they received the all-clear from health professionals, my friend was given an email to show the police when crossing local government areas (LGA) on her way to work. Tragically, their youngest daughter unexpectedly tested positive, plunging them into another round of quarantine. As they couldn't work, their savings dwindled, and they relied on close friends for groceries.

Witnessing their dire situation, an idea occurred to me one weekend. I shared it with my husband; we would venture across the LGA boundary to shop for their family. We'd prepare cultural dishes and gather essential items to support them. Looking back, it's quite amusing how we drove past LED trailers with brightly coloured messages warning us that we were leaving our LGA. We could have been fined during that time, and I couldn't help but imagine helicopters overhead and barriers across the motorway as the police conducted checks on each vehicle, seeking evidence of where the driver and passengers truly resided. We drove in silence, apprehensive of what might happen, to our destination two LGAs away to purchase the necessary ingredients.

When we picked up the meat products, our car, unfortunately, wouldn't start. The retail outlet had strict health and safety procedures in place due to the pandemic, allowing only one shopper inside at a time, mandating masks, and QR codes for entry. Seeing our predicament, one of the shop owners, recognising us as regular customers, sent his son to help us jump-start our car. Our hearts raced with gratitude as we quickly returned home, nervously listening to the car radio, half-expecting police roadblocks. That very afternoon, I began cooking a hearty meal, still having bags of groceries in the fridge. I reached out to a colleague who lived near my friend's house, asking them to deliver the food. When I called my friend to inform her of our gesture, she could hardly believe it. Instead of accepting her thanks, I expressed how grateful I was to have the opportunity to follow in my grandparents' footsteps, sharing kindness with others.

A week later, I received a call and a text message from my friend. She had received the food and was too busy enjoying it to talk to me. Eventually, my friend returned to work and I sent a gracious "you're very welcome" email. My mind was at ease, knowing that I had been able to help. Regrettably, that would be the last time I heard from their family. I have a sense that they are doing well, but I had moved on, resigning from my position. It was the last time I would step into the prison after nearly 13 years. The time had come to move forward, even though it would be a while before we could return to a semblance of normalcy after the devastating global impact of the pandemic. Nonetheless, we had survived.

What's Gang Rape?

Puberty was a nightmare and it was my virginity that seemed to be the target by the pack of dogs circling me. They could smell fresh blood and personally it was then, I realised that I held those Maori boys in such contempt. Up until that time I had seen them abuse young pakeha (white) girls in the movies on a Saturday afternoon in virtual packs. It was easy for them to overpower her to the point when one Maori boy was kissing her, another was trying to get into her pants. Short of high fiving each other for success in their conquests, it was with complete disgust that I knew some of them to be my relations.

Upon reflection I wonder if I had unknowingly set myself up for the future to view sex as a power game. I would attend parties around Scotts Ave with friends I had grown up with and now we were all teenagers. It was a rude awakening that my immaturity and alcohol did not mix and I would make decisions that would affect the rest of my life. Beneath my skin I felt the pressure and had decided to give my virginity away the first moment I could, to a complete stranger, someone who was not from our town and there was little likelihood that we would ever meet again.

I think I was only 14 when our neighbour's daughter asked if I would like to go out with her one night so she wouldn't have to go alone. I don't think she had many friends. She intended on going out to a social at the rugby club in town and there would be music and plenty of people our own age. We weren't really friends and though I had known her most of my life I felt she resented me for some reason, though I was not sure why. I had no idea she had a bottle of spirits until it was there on the table in front of me. I had never drunk alcohol before, instead preferring to enjoy music – I loved to dance.

I'm not even sure why I agreed to have a drink – perhaps it was peer pressure or maybe I just wanted to show her I was more mature than my age. The spirits went straight to my bowels, and I spent half the night in the toilet. I remember after about the fifth time on my way back to our table that I thought I saw a friend I had gone to school with. I feel embarrassed now just recalling these events. My face and my cheeks feel hot with shame.

The room had become very small with so many people as it filled toward the end of the night and the music seemed a lot louder. I had just reached my friend when, with a sickening thud, I passed out at his feet. When I came to, my friend had carried me outside to get some air, but there was someone on top of me. He was inside me and though I pleaded and pleaded with him to get off me, he just laughed with his stinky breath in my face. I was pinned down and though he was moving quickly I couldn't move – I felt like I was being held down. I started to yell at him to get off me, but suddenly another ugly face that was different from the last was inches away from my own and I started to plead for him to get off me. I couldn't breathe properly.

Just as I felt like I was drowning, I felt this load lift off me and the voice of my cousin swearing at whoever it was. "Didn't you hear me? I told you to get the hell off my cousin." I staggered up, pulled my jeans around my ankles and my cousin led me away into the darkness of the night. She lived across the park and a few streets away. I think I was in shock and could barely thank her – I had not really realised what had happened.

It didn't take long for us to get to her place. My clothes were wet, and I was covered in mud, so she told me to take a long hot shower. While I was in the shower, it was like I couldn't get the feel and smell off my skin and the tears flowed freely down my cheeks. She had phoned some of her friends to come over to hers, because she wanted to go back to the club and call those guys out. Of course, I blamed myself – how could I have been so stupid? We didn't even think of calling the police. I was a Māori girl and had been drinking underage, why on earth would they believe me? For years to come, I would struggle with my own sexuality and being creative, I understood girls could become players too … .wasn't sex about power?

At different times in my life, I would come face to face with the crime of sexual assault and was not always the victim. I was much older when my elder sister told me a story about when we lived in our family home in Scotts Ave. I remembered looking at things through the eyes of a child like when Dad was beating Mum to a pulp in the hallway, but my elder sister told me, "One night someone just snuck into our house when they were out". She said that she woke up suddenly because she felt rough cold hands inside her pajamas moving all over her body. She couldn't have been more than 10 or 11 years old.

My sister told me about this the night before she passed away. I waited and listened for her to tell me what happened next, and I believe she did not find out who it was until years later herself. She was visiting an aunty who was a seer (in our culture we also have people with supernatural gifts) and this aunty told her that she could see who the perpetrator was. It was a man (pedophile) from our own neighbourhood who had been drinking with our parents the same night and it wasn't hard for him to work out that we were home alone.

As I mentioned earlier, my eldest sister was raised by our grandparents, which may have been because our parents were so young when she was born. Mum and Dad were at school together and though Mum was older than Dad, I believe because Mum was raised for much of her childhood by her own grandparents in a small village, that Dad was more worldly. Our Mum, God bless her, was a real homebody. There came a time, when Mum and Dad's marriage ended, that our grandparents on Mum's side sent her away to stay with a cousin down on the South Island. She was having a breakdown and needed time, so we stayed with them in a three-bedroom home. Our grandparents worked hard to keep a roof over our heads and continue to feed us.

We had two small rooms; one was our grandparent's room and the other was usually for mum's youngest brother. We occupied a big bedroom with two single beds and one double bed that was where I usually slept. Both my sisters and my mum's youngest brother were both teenagers and I think they took turns with the other single room for privacy more than for any other reason. One night while my eldest sister slept in the single room, someone climbed in through the open window while she slept and raped her.

What's Gang Rape?

Mum's youngest brother told us the story but at the time I was much too young to realise what all the drama was about. There was always so much going on in our grandparent's house with all those teenagers in one place and when my grandmother became concerned with how withdrawn I was (because my elder sister would growl at me that I was being ungrateful) I would put on an act and try to reassure my grandmother I was fine by talking to her more. I believe our eldest sister never really got over it and in her later years would become manic depressive, living the same nightmare over and over again.

> *"Grace baffles us because it goes against the intuition that everyone has, in the face of injustice …. A price must be paid. A murderer cannot simply go free, a child abuser cannot shrug and say, "I just felt like it". A price has been paid. Grace is free only because the giver has already borne the cost rather than give up humanity."* (P Yancey, 2002)

A New Beginning in Australia

In 1981, we arrived in Australia, and it felt like we had just made a great escape from living in my in-laws' pockets. I was determined to create a new future for my family. Learning about the local area where we settled and the efficient transport system in Sydney, which, I must say, is second to none, was exhilarating. My husband and I, along with our young son, were graciously offered accommodation by our best friends who had moved here from the small town we all grew up in together just a year earlier. It didn't take long for both of us to secure jobs. I started working part-time at the local Technical College for Adult Further Education (TAFE) canteen. Two weeks after our arrival in Australia, we rented a small unit directly across the road.

As our son grew and entered preschool care, I began contemplating a return to full-time work. My husband's attitude seemed to shift dramatically. Not only did he oppose the idea of me working, but he also wanted us to have another child. Perhaps it was because he came from such a large family, totalling 14 members, each with their own, often very large, families. These were the first signs that our desires were diverging, leading us down different paths.

When I discovered his affair, I decided to leave him and live in Surfers' Paradise on the Gold Coast. On the day I left, he followed me to the airport, having purchased a ticket for himself, and sat next to me on the plane. His anger was palpable; he couldn't believe I was running away. I suppose he thought I was unaware of his infidelity, and in his anger, he struck me in the face. The passengers in the aisle seats witnessed it but chose not to intervene, saying nothing.

The pain of his betrayal cut deep, and I felt humiliated, knowing it had been going on for some time. I was working at a Data Centre in Westpac Bank, a promotion that came with rotating shifts, causing us to become like ships passing in the night. He filed for divorce through the family court, and they granted him full custody of our son because I had to work to support myself (just as my mother had done raising us herself), while his new wife would be at home with their new child.

My youngest sister, heavily pregnant at the time, was deeply upset to witness my marriage crumbling before her eyes. She cared deeply for me. Her family lived not far from our unit, and one day, she came by to find my little son playing outside, looking dishevelled and playing in just his underwear. It appeared as though no one was looking after him. She picked him up and took him home with her. On a spur-of-the-moment decision, she hopped on a plane and brought him up to Surfers' Paradise on the Gold Coast, where I was staying at the time.

Upon her return to Sydney, I called my son's father and explained what had happened, reassuring him that I would take care of our child. However, it didn't last. It was too challenging; I didn't drive and was working for the local council in a non-traditional role, part of a team raising fire hydrants in and around newly developed suburbs. My work required early hours, which meant I had to walk him to his childcare centre just after dawn, and during winter, it was cold and dark. I managed to get some help from a friend's teenage kids, but their support was inconsistent, and since we weren't blood-related, I felt I was imposing too much. Eventually, I asked his dad to come and take him because I had to admit I wasn't being a good mother, and I was not handling my own issues appropriately, often turning to alcohol and drugs to numb the pain.

When I later came down to visit my son, their unit was empty. They had moved out, and it wasn't until later that I learned his father and his new wife had managed to take my son out of Australia. She worked for the NZ passport office and had a passport made for him without my permission. My dad contacted me, telling me he had seen my son sitting in the back seat of a car owned by his family, parked outside the local bank. That was when I finally discovered that he was living back in New Zealand, and I wouldn't see him for many years.

(E) The Prodigal Son

Storm, my middle son, was diagnosed with Attention Deficit Hyperactivity Disorder (ADHD) when he was just 4 ½ years old by one of the leading paediatricians at Westmead Children's Hospital. My curiosity was piqued when I watched a documentary about children with behavioural problems on TV, and their symptoms strongly resonated with Storm's behaviour.

An Extraordinary Life

I wasted no time in scheduling an appointment for him. He had always been an incredibly curious child. To illustrate this, let me share an example:

One day, another tenant dropped a piece of candy into the bottom of a stormwater drain in the middle of the driveway outside our unit block. Storm, who was around seven or eight at the time and strong for his age, lifted the heavy 20-kilo drain cover and retrieved the candy. However, in his excitement, he dropped the cover onto his big toe, narrowly avoiding severing it entirely. We rushed him to the emergency department at the Children's Hospital as he screamed in pain, which seemed never-ending until he received a morphine shot to finally bring his agony under control. The doctors performed surgery to save his big toe, essentially reattaching it to his foot.

Once we received a confirmed diagnosis of ADHD, my life became intertwined with research. I delved into every piece of literature on ADHD, searching for answers. Storm's symptoms included impulsivity, an attention span resembling the size of a saucer, and boundless energy. However, the biggest challenge we faced was his difficulty adapting to change and staying organised. It seemed to me that doctors were too quick to prescribe medication to manage his condition, while I was in search of alternative solutions.

I was eventually compelled to put him on medication due to the rules enforced by his school. According to them, and under the pressure of his teachers and the school principal, his hyperactivity was "better managed" by using Ritalin, which is essentially an amphetamine – a highly addictive form of speed. This was to prevent him from disrupting the other children in his class who were trying to learn. I heard many other parents in his class lamenting the fact that their children deserved more recognition because they were better behaved. It was a valid point, but I understood that Storm's teacher was more motivated to reward him for good behaviour to allow the rest of the class to focus on their studies.

I once asked Storm how it felt when he took his medication before school. He described it as being like sitting in the back seat of a speeding car, looking out the window as everything outside rushed by at an incredible pace. I became actively involved at the school, volunteering in the canteen and assisting his teacher with reading classes alongside other mothers. After school, Storm and I spent time working on his reading skills and completing his homework. A few times a week and on weekends, we travelled to his various sports training sessions – he on his bike and me on my mountain bike with our baby in a seat behind me. Often, I expended an immense amount of energy, even carrying our bikes over train station platforms to catch a train to nearby suburbs to get closer to his playing fields.

Over time, I noticed that the light in Storm's eyes, the one that showed he was enjoying life, was gradually being replaced by a dullness. It was as if the medication was taking a toll on his mental health. To counteract the effects of Ritalin, he needed additional medication to help him sleep. These medications were costly, and as a single mother who did not believe in heavily sedating her child just so he could learn, I felt there had to be a better way. I believed that alternatives existed, such as allowing him to run around the school football field before class, which would help him focus and settle in class at the start of the day.

I explored several non-traditional methods outside of conventional medicine. First, we visited a chiropractor who identified coordination difficulties, neck flexor muscle weakness, and postural distortions in Storm. It was suggested that he might be suffering from mild, non-traumatic cervical vertebral dysfunction, which could be contributing to his learning difficulties. The monthly expenses for chiropractic care were significant, but I believed it was worth it at the time. Other health professionals suggested that behavioural issues in a child could be linked to events surrounding their birth. In a strange way, it made sense, given the dramatic way Storm entered the world. He was named "Storm" because I never made it to the delivery room – the doctor caught him in the hallway outside the lift on the way to the delivery suite, like a rugby player catching a football. Chiropractors who worked with children with various learning disabilities maintained that spinal adjustments were a preferable alternative to mind-altering drugs.

We also explored Eastern medicine. Storm received acupuncture treatments to open his 'chi pathways,' which were thought to help him relax and slow down. During one appointment, he looked at me with tears in his eyes, questioning what he had done wrong to endure the needles. We then considered herbal remedies, but the associated costs were prohibitive for a single mother, so I focused on managing his diet at home instead. Allergy tests revealed red flags related to certain foods and drinks, such as avoiding those with excessive sugar, like red cordial.

As I mentioned before, we utilised sports as a way to channel his excess energy. Storm played rugby, started taekwondo classes, and participated in T-ball for the Orioles during the summer. Many of his coaches marvelled at his speed and strength for his age, often awarding him medals and naming him 'Player of the Year' for his rugby team. However, registering for these activities and acquiring uniforms came at a high cost, and we had to make numerous sacrifices.

Ultimately, I agreed to have Storm participate in a Belconnen research study conducted by a psychologist, focusing on ADHD behaviours and seeking solutions to everyday problems. Unfortunately, by that time we had been addressing these behaviours on a daily basis for many years, there were no groundbreaking discoveries.

I experimented with various methods to manage his behaviour at home. I followed advice from books, using star charts for good behaviour displayed on the fridge door and providing plenty of positive reinforcement. I also attended support groups to hear how other struggling parents were coping and worked closely with his teacher. Parent-teacher interviews were challenging, but I continued my search for support and answers. Unfortunately, the answers proved elusive because the treatment pathways following an ADHD diagnosis were still in their infancy, and there was limited understanding of the condition. What worked for some children didn't necessarily work for others, making the journey all the more frustrating. My own mental health began to suffer, and in an attempt to cope, I sought counselling. Although the counsellor admired everything we had accomplished, her advice was simple: write a book about my journey. Now, with two children, I was doing everything I could to keep going, but inside, I felt like I was headed for a breakdown. So, as a last-ditch effort, I reached out to my family for help.

Storm's grandfather suggested that I send Storm to him for care to give myself some respite. However, when Storm arrived in New Zealand, another arrangement was made, and he ended up staying with my elder sister's family. They ran a Māori Kohanga Reo (pre-school) on one level of their three-story home, where they managed his behaviour without medication. Storm was seven or eight years old at the time, and his aunt's family had many members living together, including cousins around his age. This was a significant departure from his previous life in our small family unit.

I loved Storm immensely, and I knew the sacrifice I was making was necessary, but I also needed time to address my own needs. I kept telling myself that this experience would provide Storm with an opportunity to learn about his cultural heritage, and in turn, discover his own identity. From a Māori cultural perspective, I hoped to adopt a holistic healing approach – addressing his mind, body, and spirit.

In less than a month, a phone call between Storm and me changed everything. In the background, his uncle's voice was heard, saying that Storm needed to be taught a lesson for something he had done. While Storm was on the phone talking to me, my nephew punched him in the head. Both of us started to cry. Storm was being abused, and I felt helpless and guilty. It was a moment of profound failure for me.

But something incredible happened at that moment. A fire that had long lain dormant in my soul was rekindled in response to the profound injustice Storm was enduring. I knew immediately what I needed to do, and I could hear my mother's voice in my conscience, saying, "You must take care of the details". The decisions and details of those decisions came to mind quickly.

As soon as I made my decision, I knew that both my sister and brother-in-law would question why I was applying to go to university when Storm had just come into their care because I couldn't handle his behaviour. There were things I realised I could only do when he wasn't with me, and it was time for me to get to work. I cast aside my fatigue and my defeated attitude and began formulating a plan for his return. To make that plan a reality, I needed to earn money. Here are the details: we would never go hungry, never live below the poverty line, always have a roof over our heads, and in my final year at university, Storm would return to Australia. He had spent his time in New Zealand attending preschool at home.

Upon his return, Storm entered high school and went back into mainstream schooling. As part of his student enrolment, the school conducted an induction process for parents of Pacific background students. We attended a six-week course, a couple of days a week, to learn about homework expectations, uniform requirements, selecting electives, and more. What truly stood out, though, was the detailed information about their discipline process.

Storm returned fluent in Te Reo Māori and English. He would later become better at speaking Te Reo Māori than all his cousins combined. He developed a strong interest in our language, constantly asking questions and making his mark in his own competitive way as he grew up.

4

Trying to Fit

When Storm turned 14, legally considered a minor in the community and the juvenile correctional system, an incident unfolded. A friend asked him to hold his mobile phone in his man bag as they headed out for a night on the town because he had no pockets. As they passed the local mall, two policemen stopped and searched them. Storm's friend's mobile phone was stolen, and Storm was arrested. He chose not to betray his friend and remained silent, leading to his detention. It was a tragically common scenario for teenagers, unaware that loyalty can sometimes be misplaced. Storm was too young to understand his legal rights, including the importance of having a support person present during police interviews. Consequently, he was sentenced to a juvenile detention center and served time, taking the blame for his friend who never even visited him while he was incarcerated.

There is much rhetoric in law journals and public discourse about juvenile justice serving as a breeding ground for young criminals. Growing up in this environment, only the strongest survive. Those young men who are transferred to adult prisons continue to undergo transformation. I firmly believe that during this critical period, when they transition from teenagers to adults while in the company of hardened criminals in maximum security, they are at their most vulnerable. For some, it may already be too late.

Having worked in the prison industry for many years and interacted with numerous young offenders, I've seen how this environment can become their new normal. "One size fits all" programs designed to address offending behaviours for young people often fail for several reasons. The most crucial one is that UNLESS a young offender genuinely wants to change, they won't. Many Māori young offenders participate in these programs solely to secure parole. Many drop out of school prematurely, get into trouble, and have low literacy skills.

Learning styles also play a role – Māori and Pacific Island young people tend to excel in art, sports, and music. There are certainly other contributing factors, but these are the most significant ones, even without the need for supporting statistics from adult incarceration rates, which are distinct from the reasons young offenders struggle to lead law-abiding lives. Storm is now in his thirties and has spent over fourteen years of his life incarcerated.

I wrote this book because, as a mother, I often wondered what more I could have done when my son, at the tender age of 14, became entangled in the legal system and slipped through the cracks. If only I had known then what I know now. From a cultural standpoint, our eldest son takes on the family mantle after his father, representing the head of the family at specific occasions when his father is absent – such as speaking at funerals, 21st birthdays, weddings, and so forth.

Trying to Fit

Although he is loved and belongs to our family unit, he is highly influenced by our teachings, rooted in cultural values and his experiences at school. However, during his impressionable years in juvenile detention, the transition from teenager to adult, the quest for his own identity could realistically become a crossroads, an intersection. In search of belonging, he might become ensnared in recruitment campaigns for Outlaw Motorcycle Gang (OMCG) membership in groups like the Comancheros, Bandidos, Rebels, Satudarah, Lone Wolves, or even be converted to Islam and become a Muslim. If we, as his family, have lost him to forces beyond our control, he will face challenges like drugs and the ability to say NO, which have shifted from being mere temptations to formidable challenges that will reshape his future. What does this say about the direction of our next generation of young Māori males growing up in Australia?

Though I and other family members visited him in juvenile detention during that time, I couldn't visit him when he was transferred to adult prisons, where he frequently ended up due to struggles outside in the community and ongoing legal issues. It was during those earlier years that I began working as an immigration detention officer. Personally, my life and those of my family members continued to progress, but Storm remained stuck in a legal system that provided inadequate rehabilitation efforts and showed little concern for his well-being.

Unfortunately, some inmates, in my opinion, fall through the cracks due to placement issues. Many prisons, whether publicly or privately managed, were expanding, constructing new wings that accommodated additional inmates. The inmate population in Sydney surged beyond 10,000, and bed availability reached a standstill. Consequently, inmates facing minor charges sometimes waited over two years (long-term remands) as the courts faced severe backlogs.

Families often contacted me through the switchboard, seeking information about their incarcerated loved ones and wondering why they hadn't heard from them. These inquiries were complex matters that required handling with both professionalism and sensitivity, while respecting privacy, due to my extensive experience and in-depth knowledge of the prison's policies and procedures.

5

That's Called Racism

My bachelor's degree had two strands, and I was on target to complete the full sub-major in HR when I graduated in 2001. I recall a troubling incident at university that left a lasting impression on me. I had a lecturer for an HR subject, Training and Development (T&D), and from the very first moment, it was clear that he did not like me. I was puzzled as to why. His disdain became apparent when I raised my hand to answer a question he posed. His response was flippant, as if he were trying to belittle me in front of the entire class. I felt embarrassed and humiliated. That evening, I couldn't understand what I had done or said to warrant such treatment. It wasn't until I shared this story with a friend from church, who knew me well, that she said, "By the sounds of it, he's a racist". Those words hit me like a ton of bricks, and I felt as though my very skin was soiled because of the unfair treatment I had endured. Unfortunately, T&D was the only subject I failed during my three years at university, according to my transcript.

As my graduation approached, I had the opportunity to attend one last workshop on Unfair Dismissal. However, I had no idea that the facilitator of the workshop was the same lecturer from that fateful day in T&D. At the end of the workshop, my professor and I were mingling with other attendees when I came face to face with him. Over the years, I had often wondered how I would handle meeting him again. When I did, I politely asked if he remembered me, and by the look in his eye, I could tell that he did. I went on to thank him for failing me in the subject of Training and Development because it pushed me to become more dedicated and committed, and I eventually passed it the second time around.

In the years that followed, I would put all the knowledge I had gained to use, becoming a dedicated and committed trainer and mentor. In 2000, the Sydney Olympics provided the perfect opportunity to apply everything I had learned at university through hands-on experience. I was selected as an interviewer for some of the 50,000 volunteers needed throughout Sydney to support the Olympic and Paralympic Games.

My skills in people management became crucial during this once-in-a-lifetime experience, and I was asked to stay on and work for the Sydney Organising Committee for the Olympic Games (SOCOG). I was promoted to Venue Staffing Assistant Manager for the sponsor hospitality venue, all while managing the reward and recognition system (R&R) for both paid and unpaid volunteers and workers at the Sydney Olympic Park.

My primary role at SOCOG Head Office in the city involved editing the daily newsletter and overseeing the R&R system, which included organising competitions, providing up-to-date event information, creating quizzes, crossword puzzles, find-a-word games, and colouring contests. I used my colleagues as "test dummies" to ensure that all the games and puzzles I had designed would yield winners with ease once we moved on-site.

As we transitioned on-site at Sydney Olympic Park after construction was completed, our managerial team underwent training as tour guides to showcase the natural flora and fauna of the park, such as kangaroo paw plants that were specially planted to highlight the park's foundations. This park had once been a quarry where the film "Mad Max," featuring Mel Gibson, was shot, and the little green bell frog was a prominent environmental feature. We organised community events for the volunteers and held countdown ceremonies to keep them engaged. I felt alive and fulfilled like never before.

I had the opportunity to personally train most of the venue staffing team and delegate my editorial tasks. Additionally, I trained staff to create weekly volunteer rostering schedules using computer programs. I was content knowing that I had completed my tasks in a highly professional manner during such a successful Olympic Games, as evidenced by the written references from the Manager of Venue Staffing and the last day BBQ celebrations I shared with our staff. I had so much to be thankful for, and my optimism for the future was soaring. It was time for me to move forward.

6

A Can-Do Attitude

Three years after working on a temporary assignment at Parramatta Gaol, I was pleasantly surprised to be headhunted for the role of Case Management Coordinator at Parklea Correctional Centre, which was managed by the private company GEO (Global Excellence in Outsourcing). Parklea presented a new opportunity, and I was excited to embrace it fully.

To provide a bit of context, Parramatta Gaol was one of the oldest gaols in New South Wales, built during the early days of colonisation. It was constructed entirely from sandstone and housed historical landmarks such as a beautiful church, a morgue, and a round house, with inmates' initials carved into the sandstone from the time of the first fleet's arrival in Sydney. The tall boardwalks that overlooked the populated compounds, where officers would patrol with loaded rifles slung over their shoulders to ensure the security and safety of inmates and staff, added to the gaol's sense of history. Eventually, Parramatta

Gaol was transformed into a museum after closing its doors in the early 2000s.

When I received an offer from GEO, I hesitated, unsure if I was ready for the role of Case Management Coordinator. Up to that point, I had only completed two temporary assignments in Classification & Placement and hadn't yet taken on the full responsibilities of a supervisor. However, my husband's unwavering support meant the world to me, and I decided to believe in his confidence that I could excel in this role. I attended the interview with a sense of uncertainty but emerged from it with a sense of surprise. As the discussion concluded and we began to talk about salary, a number was discreetly jotted down on a post-it note and slid across the table toward me.

Upon reviewing the number, I realised that it wasn't significantly higher than my current pay. I was considering taking on a much greater role and more significant responsibilities, including managing a team of two staff members. I declined the initial offer, at which point the HR Manager asked what I had in mind in terms of compensation. To be honest, I hadn't done my research to determine the appropriate "going rate" for this position. So, I added a few extra zeros to the figure and agreed to a 2% annual increase for the first three years. The HR Manager informed me that they would need to consult with the Executive Operational Manager (EOM) but assured me they would have an answer after lunch.

To my astonishment, I was informed that I had been successful and was asked to start work in two weeks. The HR Manager revealed that when they contacted the EOM, the response was, "Pay her whatever she wants". With this opportunity, the real work began as I assessed the state of affairs within our area of specialisation.

A Can-Do Attitude

I discovered that the two staff members assigned to assist me had received training from another coordinator at Corrective Services. As I delved into my report analysis to make an assessment about how far behind we were, I realised there was substantial work to be done, particularly in the training and development of my own team. I initiated a mentoring program to ensure they could contribute effectively to our objectives. In our office, I implemented spreadsheets to track our key performance indicators and established an auditing system to create a paper trail that we could continuously refine and enhance.

While it may sound straightforward, this was a pivotal time to work within our parameters, add value to our core workload, and demonstrate that we were an integral part of the gaol's operations. Our primary goal was to ensure that our processes and recommendations offered by the team for Classification & Placement were responsible, accountable, and transparent, focusing on procedural fairness since the online assessment was primarily about the inmates. We aimed to maintain the integrity of our audit processes.

Each area of the main gaol presented unique challenges in terms of how both custodial and non-custodial staff carried out their duties. My primary interest was in understanding the practices of custodial staff. For example, there was a works release unit where eligible inmates could work outside the correctional centre as part of a reintegration program. By closely observing and consulting with the manager, supervisor, and experienced custodial staff, I gained insights into the eligibility criteria and their processes. This information allowed me to tailor our case management processes and adapt how my team interviewed inmates housed in that specific area.

I recognised the importance of professional development for my expanding team, which would eventually grow from two to ten members. I customised my mentoring strategies to build relationships with each staff member, transitioning from purely human resources interactions to deeper personal connections. Effective communication and participation within the team, whether as an observer or team member rather than a leader, allowed me to evaluate how my staff conducted inmate interviews and interacted with individuals on a personal level. I provided them with informational pamphlets and answered their questions, fostering an environment for training and mentorship. Additionally, this approach provided valuable insights into improving the layout of our satellite offices around the gaol, ensuring they were equipped with the necessary IT infrastructure to streamline our work and enhance the safety and security of my team.

A Can-Do Attitude

Cavalry Has Arrived

During the second COVID-19 lockdown at the gaol, a directive was issued to have all non-essential staff vacate the premises. The pandemic was taking a significant toll on both inmates and staff, and in response, a field hospital was set up, reminiscent of the *MASH* series on TV. Doctors from a nearby hospital close to the city arrived to tend to our inmates infected with the virus, and their numbers swelled to nearly 200. In this challenging environment, I contacted the governor and made the decision not to leave the site. My rationale was rooted in the fact that many of my team members were transitioning back to their custodial officer duties to bolster their ranks. The ranks had been thinning as several staff who had previously worked in hospital escorts with inmates were now stationed in COVID-19 wards, returning to work while exhibiting symptoms.

It was evident that the Commissioner of Corrective Services was providing instructions to all staff across the state via an Emergency Command Post. The goal was to effectively manage the rapidly changing landscape, a scale of crisis we had never encountered before. The remaining non-custodial staff members were relocated outside the main gate of the gaol, and there were good reasons for this decision. One was pregnant, another was undergoing surgery, and yet another had a wedding planned, which had been postponed twice already due to the pandemic. This arrangement allowed them to continue contributing their skills and supporting operations, ensuring they continued to receive their paychecks. Many non-essential staff members were compelled to take accrued recreational leave at a time when travel was restricted, and the only outdoor activity permitted was an hour of exercise. Shopping centres were largely closed, except for grocery stores, and the most absurd aspect of the situation was the hysteria over toilet paper. People reacted with anxiety and frustration, creating quite a spectacle, but that's a story for another time.

As the second lockdown eventually came to an end, I received another job offer, this time in New Zealand. At the time, I believed that this might be the solution to my predicament. I could relocate my family, including my grandkids, and finally return home. However, my husband had different plans. By that point, I had lived in Australia for 40 years and had achieved many of the goals I had set when I first arrived. I had climbed the career ladder and was earning a six-figure income. I had also raised my children to the best of my ability, ensuring they never went a day without shelter or food.

So, I found myself in a position where I needed to reassess my situation. After concluding my work at the gaol, I made the difficult decision not to accept the new job offer because my husband was unwilling to move, and I couldn't imagine surviving without him—my rock. Instead, I would need to explore other avenues to work and secure a future for my grandsons. I knew I needed a Master Plan and began making my initial decisions when I collected my superannuation. Trust had always been a complex issue for me, shaped by past relationships. To say I had trust issues would be an understatement. While I typically lived in the present, at that moment, I found myself transported back into the past.

As I found myself at this juncture, having spent my entire life working, I now faced the profound moment of distributing my hard-earned legacy to my three children. The circumstances had changed due to COVID-19; they wouldn't have to wait until I was no longer around. My children and grandchildren needed these resources immediately to sow the seeds of their own future. I felt an overwhelming sense of gratitude that I could provide this for them. One consequence of a lifetime of work is that my mind refused to settle. Readers will witness how I pondered over matters and found resolutions through the kind of follow-up action that defines my personality.

My retirement strategy began to take shape. Despite my lifelong love of learning, one might assume it would be easy for me, but it was not. My family always came first, and I was catching up on things when I decided to write this book. Initially, my husband, who knows me well, saw that it was driving me a bit "around the bend". With all the free time on my hands, I pondered how I could continue to be productive. After a few false starts, I began to think more clearly, aided by his nudges in the right direction, of course.

My daughter and grandkids had moved into their new forever home. She had diligently saved for a deposit and had stayed with us during the lockdowns, with our support. The boys were about to start at a new school, and the younger one (though we adore them both, he's the "joy of our heart") was beginning big school that year. I would rush to their house early in the mornings since my daughter still worked varying hours and needed our assistance. The boys needed a routine, and grandmothers like me, who have a history of working and being somewhat "process-oriented," have their own way of doing things, akin to a sergeant major in the Army. Well, that approach worked only until they started answering back – I can almost hear you laughing!

I've worked with hardened criminals and trained and mentored staff to think and act as I do. Yet, here were my grandsons, testing the very ground I walked on. God love them, but I was trying to keep the little hair I had left on my head from being pulled out by the roots, trying to find ways to get them to do what I wanted. Through this experience, I realised I had difficulty "bending". All those years of bodybuilding taught me about technique but not necessarily about knowing when to yield – and that wasn't one of my strong suits.

We eventually reached a showdown, or perhaps a standoff would be a better description. Once they both began talking to me as if I were the hired help, that was likely the last straw. Especially when they complained about how old they were and how they could manage to get themselves to school without my assistance. I had a conversation with my husband and daughter. We decided to see how they managed on their own. If you can picture me with my fingers crossed behind my back while saying that I hope it works out, then you'll understand that I'm not the kind of grandmother who easily lets go of the reins.

Fostering a Culture of Respect

In 2013, I became a part of a diverse community group united by a shared mission: helping young people. My journey had commenced long before this, but I'll delve into that backstory later. During this period, I received a program crafted by a highly educated and influential Māori individual, whom I am proud to call a close friend, Dr. Ben Pittman (deceased). Dr. Pittman, holding a PhD from UTS, an MFA with Honours, and the ONZM distinction (Officer of the NZ Order of Merit in 2021 for services to Māori & Art), and I had both served on several community committees, culminating in the Sydney Marae Fundraising Appeal Executive Committee.

Around the same time, I crossed paths with Mick Ainsworth, a renowned barrister with two decades of experience, whose work with young offenders of Pacific Island heritage had captured my attention. Over coffee meetings, it quickly became evident that Mick shared the same passion for our journey.

Completing our group was Mr. Mano Tairi, Chairman of the Sydney Marae Committee, whose involvement added a unique dimension to our shared goal of assisting young people of Māori and Pacific Island heritage. Our committee convened at various venues, indulging in food and drinks while crafting plans. Our discussions were often animated. I would absorb the invaluable insights provided by these experts—individuals who were not only professionals but also authorities in their respective fields. My role was to take diligent notes, ensuring we had a clear path forward and a roadmap for tasks to be researched, completed, or presented at our next meeting.

The program, developed and spearheaded by Ben, who also served as the CEO of a training organisation, was the fruit of our deliberations. At the inception of my venture, I made a strategic decision to change its name due to availability. While we initially intended to introduce this program as a face-to-face course within Corrective Services under the banner of MANA PASIFIKA, circumstances prompted a shift in our approach. In response to the evolving needs of our community and the constraints imposed by COVID-19, I opted to take the program online and into the wider community, rebranding it as MANA TANGATA, which translates to "People of Respect".

From its inception, the MANA TANGATA program aimed to be a local court initiative for young offenders, enriched with cultural content and practices designed to empower and engage these youths, enabling them to shape their own futures. What does this future entail, you might ask? For these young individuals, it could involve meeting their life partner, starting a family, becoming leaders, pursuing high-powered careers, or even exploring the world—choices and opportunities abound. In the words of the Māori proverb "Ka hao te rangatahi," which means "the new net goes fishing," it is a call to action, suggesting that it is time for young people to take charge. Just as social media platforms attract followers, I leave it to the reader's imagination whether it is fitting for me to produce session plans and manage an online program.

Reflecting on our early efforts to secure funding for the program within Corrective Services, it's apparent that we may have been somewhat short-sighted. Why would Corrective Services support an initiative aimed at reducing the number of clients or potential inmates when their core business revolves around housing, feeding, and rehabilitating inmates? Māori and Pacific Island inmates, while often grouped together, constitute a minority within the broader population of New South Wales, which currently stands at approximately 10,500. However, my initial research revealed that among people from the Pacific Islands (and I say this to mean Polynesians, Micronesians & Melanesians)—Tongans, Samoans, Cook Islanders, Fijians, and Māori—it was the Tongan inmates serving notably longer sentences for severe offenses.

There were two programs I was able to action, one which was the first of its kind in the state of NSW - a bone carving class together with an action plan to encourage a small group of Māori inmates to be trained in the art of carving an item of "cultural significance" to be displayed at the opening of a new Cultural centre within the gaol. The course was recognised by TAFE (Technical and Further Education) and the inmates received a Statement of Attainment. A dear friend offered to voluntarily come into the gaol and train these inmates how to carve.

The second program involved convening a meeting between the representatives from NSW Rugby League Referees Association and senior management members to discuss ways for inmate to participate in a program that would enable them to complete the theoretical underpinnings to a certificate IV in Refereeing (there was a crucial shortage of referees out in the community - soccer, rugby league, rugby etc). Linking together a work stream from within the main gaol having completed the theoretical stream now eligible inmates can be moved to the Pre-Release program to complete the practical components out in the community on day release from the gaol. Inmates would have a paying job as a referee upon release.

I want to express my gratitude to the Pacific Island Program (now known as PIP) and its founder, Weber Roberts. I first crossed paths with Weber at a football game where his son was playing, and we found ourselves seated in the stands. Having heard much about the successful Pacific Island Program (PIP) run out of the Mt Druitt Probation and Parole Unit in 2005, I was eager to learn if I could facilitate such a program. Weber candidly labeled me an "intellectual dummy," a remark that, while initially startling, was accurate. At that time, lacking skills but brimming with enthusiasm, he was in the process of completing his PhD, and my request did not align with his priorities.

Little did I realise that his seemingly offhanded comment would significantly influence the path I would take to prove to myself that I could achieve this. But before delving into that, let me summarise the statistics derived from an assessment conducted in the initial years of PIP.

CRES Evaluation Statistics

Mt Druitt COS Pacific Island Program:

Fostering a Culture of Respect

Groups facilitated between June 2004 – 2007: 292 offenders completed PIP

Breakdown of offenses:

General violence/assault - 47%

Domestic violence – 26%

Driving offenses – 14%

Robbery and stealing – 13%

Number of programs increased each year:

2004 – 4

2008 – 8

In 2005, of those who completed the program, 11% had committed another offense, and 1% faced breach action.

In contrast, offenders who failed to complete the program had reoffending rates of 31.4% and breach action initiated in 25.71% of cases.

Recidivism rates:

2004 = 31%, 2005 = 27%, 2006 = 23%, 2007 = 3 (raw figures)

The program's goal is to reduce recidivism to under 20%.

The 2005 CRES evaluation supported the PIP's effectiveness, emphasising the incorporation of cultural values and beliefs into an offender management program. The success prompted referrals from other COS offices within the western Sydney region and local magistrates, making it a parole condition for Pacific parolees. However, the program's growing profile strained staff and resources, leading to substantial pressure.

As early as 2008, a short-sighted response hindered the potential expansion of PIP into other areas. Despite its success and positive impact on the Pacific community, opportunities for similar programs in Campbelltown and Liverpool COS areas were missed.

Acknowledgments are due to the staff from the Mt Druitt COS unit, particularly Phyllis Zinghini, for her contribution, aiding Pacific parolees in filling out applications for courses at the local TAFE, enhancing their employability skills through education.

Further recognition goes to the staff at SWAHS (Southwest Area Health Service), particularly Alicia Peacock, whose years of service combined Pacific learning styles with programs covering Alcohol and Other Drugs, domestic violence, and local police visits. This broadened the knowledge of program participants.

In 2023, after nearly 13 years of working within the jail system, I had the pleasure of meeting Weber again in retirement. It was deeply satisfying to thank him for his positive contribution to the Pacific community through the development of the PIP at Mt Druitt COS unit. I also conveyed how he influenced my career path, leading to mentorship by two remarkable Māori mentors, solidifying my credibility.

Fostering a Culture of Respect

My academic journey at the University of Western Sydney Nepean, where I graduated in 2000 with a Bachelor's Degree in Business, equipped me with critical thinking skills, strategic planning, and enhanced analytical abilities. This theoretical education underpinned my human resource skills, complementing my experience at Parklea Correctional Centre. Over eleven years, my team and I achieved outstanding results in the Classification and Placement department, reaching 99% in 2010 and maintaining 100% for the remaining decade whilst working for a private company, GEO, which demanded excellence.

The tough nature of this role compared to working in the public sector of Corrective Services was evident. My first mentor, the Training Manager Garry Campbell at Villawood Immigration Detention Centre (VIDC), guided me through various aspects of training, emphasising the importance of assessments and evaluations. This knowledge proved invaluable when I became his Training Assistant for a six-week Pre-Service course for new recruits.

My second noteworthy mentor, Dr. Benjamin Pittman, facilitated the Presidential project establishing a partnership between the Rotary Club of Sydney CBD (2009-2010) and St. Andrew's Cathedral School. This initiative focused on the Māori Youth in the World - Standing Tall Leadership program. The support of Sydney Marae Incorporated was also acknowledged in this three-day program based on cultural values and principles. Serving as a presenter/observer, I admired Dr. Pittman's exceptional training skills, and over the years, we developed a strong friendship.

An Extraordinary Life

He's My Soulmate

The week before I met him, I made the acquaintance of a psychologist from NZ at a HR conference who knew of him as she worked in the same correctional centre. She had talked him up as an up-and-coming unit manager but pointed out he liked to be known by his nickname. Unfortunately, meeting him for the first time was nerve-racking. I was trying so hard to make a good impression and put on my biggest smile. I was disappointed that when I said hello, he just barked at me because I had called him the wrong name – Charles – instead of Junior, which he was affectionately known as by his family and friends. I didn't find him affectionate at all.

He was, after all, walking onto my turf. This was my centre that I was protecting these past years and I hoped that our new Operations Manager was going to be the real deal and sort out the many staffing issues we were experiencing. While I was going through my pre-service training our centre had the biggest escape ever from a detention centre in Australia; 33

detainees escaped through a tunnel dug underneath the centre and linked up to water pipes that led out to the main road. Media sensationalised our every move and we became high profile because the private company I was working for, whose parent company was based in the USA, and our immigration policy was still under development – a grey area. Unlike corrections, their policies were in plain black and white.

I believe we became friends because, although I didn't know it at the time, we were born in the same year. He's just a little older than I, but we enjoy the same music and watched the same movies growing up. We are both of Māori descent so we share the same values and he spoke Māori fluently – though I have only a working knowledge that my mother taught me as I was growing up; my mum had been severely punished for speaking in our native tongue at school. But the most important factor that drew us together, is that we share the same sense of humour. I would bump into him outside the lunchroom, and we would laugh together as I would tell him a story about funny incidents about our staff as we got to know each other and learned about each other's background. He had a 19-year career in corrections and was poached by my company, who was looking for someone like him – a Unit Manager with strong operational skills in policy and strong management skills, though it was his budgeting skills and the way in which he managed the staff that gained my admiration.

The first night he asked me out, we were both attending a work event and I actually turned him down, citing that I was busy installing a new computer I was leasing. He looked at me with absolute disbelief and told me it was like I was handing him a challenge, so when I told him I didn't like the idea of going out with the boss he casually said "I was sacked" and he would pick me up at 8pm. I worked as a detention officer for four years and he earnt my respect as I watched our centre become self-sufficient and staffing become better utilised. With such tender and constant loving care, I was finally able to surrender my heart and quell the demons long enough to take a risk on this man who made me feel his equal. I was totally captivated and when he left Villawood and went back over to corrections, I followed him.

F) Fire at the Detention Centre

The afternoon was growing late, and excitement filled the air. New Year's Eve was upon us, and for the first time, I wasn't on shift. I hoped we would head into the city together to watch the festivities unfold. I arrived at the centre to wait for him until his shift ended. While I was waiting, I knew my cousin had arranged for a karaoke machine to be set up in Stage 1 compound, so the detainees could have some fun. I decided to go down and see the entertainment.

I was in civilian clothes, not in uniform, and even got up to sing a number with my cousin. I greatly admired her selflessness; catering for the families was her passion. It was never any trouble for her to provide clothing for the children, furniture for their dwellings, or a shoulder to cry on. She was the kind of person who took her role as programs officer seriously, and her tenacity was truly admirable. She was there for the staff as well, and we all loved her for her contagious enthusiasm.

During my shifts, I often found myself going out of my way to assist her with her clothing donations from the community. We sorted, washed, and organised piles of clothing in various sizes, both for adults and children based on their ages. These piles were stored away until they were needed.

I had planned to visit Stage 2 when things quieted down, but my plans took an unexpected turn when I arrived at the visiting area. It was a clear night, and looking back at Stage 1, I couldn't ignore the ominous glow. The situation quickly escalated into an emergency—a fire had broken out.

I found myself, along with other officers, rushing to assist. The radio traffic was frantic, and I heard a desperate call for help. I immediately sought out the external perimeter officer who was conducting a security check around Stage 1. He was young and clearly overwhelmed, his wide eyes and rapid speech revealing his fear. I asked him for the keys to the external vehicle and jumped in. I sped to the other side, where I realised that most of the dining room had already been consumed by flames. But the immediate threat was right in front of me.

I turned on the vehicle's high beams, shining them directly on the fences. In the dim light, I could see detainees trying to scale the fences in an attempt to escape. One detainee even had a suitcase in his hand while desperately trying to climb. It was our duty to prevent them from getting away. Amidst the noise of the alarms and the crackling of the fire, I realized that we needed to get them off the fences as quickly as possible. Since I didn't have a radio, I made eye contact with my partner, who informed us that the request to use munitions had been declined. However, we could pick up rocks and began throwing them to deter the detainees from climbing further.

In the chaos, an excavator had previously been working in the area, leveling the roadway for our vehicles, leaving a large supply of rocks at our feet. We shouted at the detainees, making them the target of our throws. The sound of alarms was deafening, and we could hear the fire trucks and a fleet of police vehicles approaching from the next suburb. No permission had been given to enter the centre, and we soon heard on the radio that some staff were locked in the control room within Stage 1, as the riot had erupted in full swing. A vehicle from within the compound seemed to be attempting to ram the gates to get out, which was surprising since an express order had been given earlier that week to prevent staff from parking their personal vehicles within the gates. The gates remained unyielding, and the police cars surrounded the fences, their sirens wailing and headlights blazing, prepared for action.

Before long, we heard instructions given to the staff inside, ordering them to evacuate and lead the detainees away from the fire. The fire trucks' hoses were directed at the flames from outside the fences, but radio traffic revealed another life-threatening situation at Stage 3—a hostage crisis.

I returned to the Transport and Escort (T&E) buildings at the corner of the site, where many staff members had gathered to assist. Some of them were in evening attire, having been at dinner with their families when they heard the sirens from the police cars. They kissed their family's goodbye and rushed to the scene.

Soon, senior management and representatives from Immigration arrived at T&E to assess the situation. My partner joined me, and he began briefing the team, outlining the plans for transferring detainees from Stage 1 to the management unit in Stage 3. With the fire crews now outside and a sense of camaraderie settling in, we wished them a Happy New Year, appreciating their efforts. We also extended our gratitude to the police units that had responded.

I was tasked with driving a van down to Stage 1 as part of the movement plans that were being implemented. After being granted access by a gate officer, I waited for the detainees to be escorted into the vehicle by the staff. Once they were securely inside, we awaited instructions from the internal gate officer to provide safe egress to Stage 3. I couldn't tell how many vans were tasked for the remaining detainees, but I remained focused on the task at hand.

I observed my cousin, who was no taller than 5 foot, taking charge of the gates, ensuring they were swiftly opened and closed, leaving no room for any unauthorised access. She made her instructions clear and unwaveringly carried them out to the best of her abilities. The night was long and exhausting, and once all the moves were completed, I searched for a quiet spot to get some sleep. With the dawn and the rising sun, the steam from the fire in Stage 1 created an eerie atmosphere. The smoke lingered in the air, and the weight of the night's events became apparent.

A debriefing would occur during the shift change, as the day staff received information and an overview of the night's events. Step-down procedures would be implemented, with a focus on the tasks for the new day.

Stage 1 was cordoned off, and only the external perimeter officer was permitted in the area, liaising with Stage 2 to monitor security checks. Senior management, senior police, and fire sergeants would assess the damage, a process that would take some time. Stage 2 staff would need to provide accommodation to detainees from Stage 1 in the general population housing.

The hostage situation at Stage 3 was resolved successfully, but the staff member involved would require ongoing counselling and a medical checkup to ensure her safety and well-being. The alleged instigators suspected of starting the fire(s) in Stage 1 were being managed in Stage 3 Management unit in segregation. Interviews and decisions about potential charges would follow investigations.

The internal staff from Stage 1 provided a harrowing account of how a detainee had managed to steal the keys to the vehicle parked in the compound, which was used to ram the gates. Thankfully, no detainees escaped or were harmed in the fire, but the cleanup, demolition, and reconstruction costs were expected to run into hundreds of thousands of dollars. The news quickly made its way to the media, with helicopters taking aerial shots of the ruins.

On New Year's Day, we slept through the day and returned to our shift to find that the situation was being managed as well as could be expected. A few years later, the external perimeter officer passed away due to a Coca-Cola addiction, as he was diabetic. My cousin also passed away, and I wanted to include her in my story to honour her extraordinary strength, heart, and selflessness. She was my superhero, and I will never forget her.

(G) Moving Forward

He tendered for the role and was successful in gaining a position in a non-custodial middle level management role of Deputy Manager of Classification for Corrective Services within Classification and Placement, a branch quite separate from the gaols, although their core workload was to work within the gaols around the State. He was sponsored for this role by a renowned superintendent of many years with a wealth of experience, knowledge and skill and in my opinion innovative insight. Memorably, one of the perks he received during this time was a personal invitation from the Commissioner of Corrective

Services requesting his attendance on a Sydney Harbour cruise for all the Pacific Managers from NZ, Fiji, Tonga, Samoa, and the Cook Islands.

He walked in like a 'diamond in the rough', relatively unknown to the other rank and file Deputy Managers, and made his mark early as his policy and procedures manual literally became his bible, and proceeded to organise staff in one of only two large remand reception gaols in Sydney. He led and participated with his staff on case management teams, interviewing inmates in crucial decision making to place the inmates to their gaols of classification with an appropriate security rating to undertake employment and participate in programs to address their offending behaviour(s).

His qualifications gained throughout an established career in NZ corrections – which began in 1986, and by 1995 saw him appointed OIC of courts, in 1997 appointed National Escort Coordinator, 2000 Unit Manager, 2001 Rosters Coordinator, 2002 Policy and Procedures reviewer and later in 2002 appointed Operations Manager at VIDC – held him in good stead and his work ethic came to be admired by the staff he worked with during these early years. In fact, he and his team won an award for excellence notably to a level never reached again by the C&P branch. A rotating roster saw the very few deputy C&P managers placed to cover clusters of gaols to include regional gaols as well.

Over time, however, the upper echelon of senior management within the gaols saw the empowerment of some very knowledgeable and experienced women rise through the ranks as well as external appointments of business leaders from leading agencies. There was a changing perspective about the way in which middle management roles were decided, with lateral transfers of staff who literally stuffed up in an area (jobs for the boys) as a second opportunity to do better elsewhere. The decision-making powers were left in the hands of senior staff, who had an entourage of followers due to their overwhelming influence, when it came time for promotions and appointments for existing custodial staff to climb the ladder.

The impact became rather concerning because now who would be confident that a promotion to another role was made on its merits. The ensuing impact on workplace culture within the gaols was that it became quite polluted, and affected mentoring relationships. A culture change was sorely needed as it became hostile at Parklea Correctional Centre where the rank-and-file members began to strike and union representatives wanted their demands heard. They won the battle but at the end of the day they lost the war. The damage was irreparable. Ultimately the government decided the public service management of Parklea CC was to be tendered out and in 2009 it was taken over by a private company.

In my opinion another poignant example of this corrosive influence was when he tried to have his NZ certificates in Offender Management recognised as prior learning. Although he attained the highest levels, it did not bode well for an organisation where the gap between protecting the competing interests and wages of their highest level of senior custodial staff over the non-custodial appeared to be ever widening.

Indeed, once the Commissioner retired, a revamp of the HR processes to become more inclusive has seen the changing roles and movement of the female custodial staff into specialised areas like the C&P branch, rather than working within the gaols to conduct an ongoing review of its policies and procedures manual and its core workload due to the evolving nature of their processes. This domain, once held exclusively by non-custodial staff to maintain the objectivity of the C&P processes, was infiltrated to allow a more responsible approach to be transparent and accountable. This subsequently protected the integrity of programs for the provision of a genuine rehabilitative offer as the political and societal shifts encroached on the ever-decreasing annual corrections budget and a change in government policy to be focused on reducing reoffending.

With these shifts came an expectation by the C&P branch that he would train more CSNSW Deputy Managers with his expertise, and abhorrently they would collect $40,000 more per year for doing the same job – those entitled and greedy administrators of a broken system. With the shift, redemption was also achieved with the introduction of an improved Policy and Procedures Manual. This finally made full realisation of the policies to the processes and thus responsibility, accountability and transparency for all levels of staffing, but in particular seniors.

There were moments throughout our work lives when we would collaborate effectively, forming a formidable team. I deeply respected his principled nature and valued his unwavering mentorship. Beyond our professional lives, we carried our work home with us—this commonality had been a bond since the early days of our relationship. However, I observed a transformation in his demeanour due to the perceived unfairness of the situation. While he could have easily succumbed to bitterness, I intervened to alter the narrative. I consistently questioned him about how he could improve the C&P processes, rather than dwelling on the actions of the staff he felt had betrayed him. Indeed, his role became redundant, and he became a casualty of the shifting landscape.

When I secured my position at the privately managed gaol in Parklea CC, he was already serving as the Deputy Manager for Corrective Services, a level above me. At the time, I had no inkling of what lay ahead and how it would impact my role in C&P, for which I remain eternally grateful. I recollected our past conversations and, when it made sense to me, I laboured diligently for the next twelve and a half years to implement the necessary changes from the very beginning.

When the time came, he was offered voluntary redundancy after ten years of service with Corrective Services, a decision he embraced without hesitation. While I worked at Parklea Correctional Centre (PCC), I was often asked whether he would consider returning to work for the privately managed gaol, coincidentally the same company we had both previously worked for, managing Villawood Detention Centre. Over time, private companies signed contracts that led GEO to shift away from managing detention services and transition into managing correctional facilities. In the early 2000s, they assumed responsibility for one of the largest interstate correctional centres, under a ground-breaking 25-year contract, touted as the longest of its kind. It included a 'payment by results' component based on improved reintegration outcomes and associated reductions in reoffending. Ravenhall's strong emphasis on rehabilitation and reintegration is evident through its offering of over 100 evidence-based programs (GEO website).

Matariki (new public holiday in NZ)

MATARIKI marked our visit to New Zealand after the international borders finally reopened following the COVID-19 pandemic that spanned 2020-2021. Our journey had been planned during the lockdown period and held a top spot on our bucket list.

My husband was eager to seize the opportunity to share the knowledge about Matariki that his father had passed down to him during his upbringing, with his own nephews and nieces. My husband and his father had participated in numerous Matariki events before his father's passing over twenty years ago. This special occasion marks the New Year in the Māori calendar. Symbolised by the reappearance of the Matariki star cluster in our night sky, it's a time to reflect on the past year, celebrate the present by honouring those who have passed on, gather knowledge about festivities, sow seeds for new crops, and sometimes compose and sing waiatas (songs).

Like a Boss

I had journeyed all the way from New Zealand to chase my dreams, to live the life I aspired to. My foremost desire was to work, so I embarked on computer courses in a field that piqued my interest. I enrolled in a correspondence course, but with a young child at home, finding the time to study proved challenging, and it eventually fell by the wayside. I then turned to night classes at the nearest high school, and there, I finally found what I had been searching for. However, it would be several years before I would summon the courage to return to formal education.

After completing a TAFE course designed for women seeking to re-enter the workforce, I made the bold decision to apply to university as a mature-age student.

Doubts filled my mind. What if I wasn't good enough? I hadn't even completed high school, and I had spent nearly five years away from the world of academia. I was somewhat naive, a fact that became glaringly evident on my very first day at university as I followed the trail of yellow arrows to locate my classes. The truth was that, while growing up, the idea of attending university never crossed my mind or that of my friends. It seemed like something reserved for those from affluent families. It was only when I discovered I could apply for HECS and not have to save up for tuition that I dared to dream of higher education.

My initial year at university involved revisiting many foundational subjects, which I had already covered as introductory courses at TAFE. Nevertheless, I remained undeterred and, eventually, chose to change my field of study entirely, finding a better fit in Human Resource Management and Industrial Relations (HRM/IR).

In later years, I would reflect on how my mother had instilled resilience in me and served as a role model throughout my life. There came a time when the strength of our family, including my mother, my little sister, and myself, was put to the test.

I was in the prime of my health, as I had always made it a priority to look after myself while raising my children on my own. A recent Facebook post summed it up well: "I work hard because I can't screw it up; I've got nobody to fall back on. I am the backup." My children practically grew up in the local gym, where I worked out three days a week.

My time was divided between my son's school, where I helped with reading classes and worked in the canteen during lunch hours. However, a routine visit to the doctor for my annual pap smear led to unexpected news. I was diagnosed with stage 4 cervical cancer. This might have halted others in their tracks, but I moved forward fearlessly. I consulted a gynecologist who confirmed the initial diagnosis, and I scheduled the laser treatment that ultimately saved my life.

Sadly, my mother and my little sister faced a different fate. Both needed to undergo full hysterectomies due to cancer, but thankfully, they both survived the surgeries. My mother expressed relief at no longer needing the physical attributes necessary for childbirth, as she had already blessed our family with six natural births. She marvelled at the intricate design of our womanly bodies, citing Psalm 139.

Regrettably, my little sister's ordeal continued. The cancer spread throughout her lower body and into her stomach, requiring radiography using gamma rays or similar ionizing radiation to view the internal form of her cancer. Her treatment was meant to be a finite process, but due to a staff change, she ended up enduring excessive radiation exposure, causing her bowel to partly melt into other organs.

In a race against time, a professor in her field operated on her bowel, but not before significant damage had been done. She lost half of her bowel's functionality, leading to bouts of uncontrollable, foul-smelling acid discharge and an urgent need to find the nearest restroom at any given moment. This condition severely restricted her daily routines, such as shopping or paying bills, effectively robbing her of the freedom she deserved.

Furthermore, she struggled with an inability to eat certain foods and spent countless hours each night trying to vomit them up. Sleep eluded her as she grappled with an unfixable condition that she never learned to cope with.

One fateful night, my sister made a heartbreaking call. She asked my husband and me to visit her for a conversation about her plan. Tragically, her plan involved ending her own life, as she could no longer bear the struggle. Several years prior, she had come to Australia from her hospital bed in New Zealand, following her terminal illness diagnosis, at my insistence, so that I could care for her and her children. Her husband, unable to accept her cancer diagnosis, remained in denial and was left behind in New Zealand.

Those years spent together were filled with wonderful memories, with lots of laughter. My sister possessed a kind and caring soul, radiating beauty both inside and out.

Next Generation Leaders

Māori and Pacific Island inmates experience one of the highest recidivism rates, often returning to incarceration within two years of their release. This perspective is rooted in my observations and the responses I've gathered through cultural assessments conducted with inmates from these specific backgrounds during my tenure at a maximum-security correctional facility.

Young offenders from these cultural backgrounds often displayed a sense of remorselessness, justifying their criminal activities as a means of survival, either to put food on the table or because they believed the victim's property was insured and their losses would be reimbursed through insurance claims.

Crimes of various types were committed for a multitude of reasons. Over my years in the industry, I began to wonder whether some of these individuals were coerced into criminal activities, particularly drug-related offenses, due to their physical strength and aggressiveness. The scenario often unfolded where the drug dealer, positioned at the back of the courtroom, escaped severe sentencing, while the "muscle" received the brunt of the punishment.

Employment opportunities for young people from these cultural backgrounds often led them to labour-intensive industries with low wages, such as process work. In essence, their families typically hailed from lower socioeconomic backgrounds, and they had limited access to higher education. Unfortunately, young offenders from these backgrounds were sometimes misjudged as lacking the intelligence to secure better-paying jobs.

Many young offenders from these cultural backgrounds participated in programs aimed at addressing their offending behaviour within the Corrective Services system. However, these programs were often seen as generic and not genuinely rehabilitative. Completion was sometimes motivated solely by the desire for parole, rather than a genuine commitment to change.

Until recently, New Zealand citizens residing in Australia were ineligible to apply for Centrelink payments. However, there have been changes in recent years that expanded eligibility for childcare benefits to include them.

(H) Deporting the Cohort

Over the past couple of years, the government has been deporting non-Australian citizen inmates sentenced to serve over one year in custody. During the COVID lockdowns, due to travel restrictions, many of these deportees were temporarily relocated to detention centres until international borders reopened. These deportees faced a wait of over two years before they could return to their home countries.

What had not been previously considered is the impact on the families left behind while these deportees are unable to re-enter the country. In most cases, the deportee serves as the family's primary breadwinner, and the family must make significant adjustments to their lives to remain in Australia. One poignant example is as follows:

In a documentary on 501s (as per the Migration Act Sec 501 Deportation Policy), a young man, despite being deported, possessed valuable skills as a scaffolder. He continued to provide for his family from afar, eventually establishing a scaffolding company. Yet, when he sought employees for his business, he found that there were so many 501 deportees that he ended up with enough staff to manage three scaffolding companies. He became a successful businessman, demonstrating that not all deportation stories end in despair.

However, not all deportation stories have such a positive outcome. I had a friend who worked as a custodial officer and kept an eye on two young New Zealand girls in the community. Both had run afoul of the law, and the elder sister was deported. Raised in Australia, they had no ties to the New Zealand community. Even before the younger sister could be sentenced, immigration deported both of them. With no support network in New Zealand, they found themselves seeking refuge in a house slated for demolition. Tragically, one of them died as a result. This incident had a profound impact on my friend, who had a sister living nearby and who ultimately decided to leave her job at the correctional facility, citing this tragedy as one of the reasons for her departure.

During my time at the correctional facility, I took it upon myself to visit these inmates and provide them with information booklets supplied by the New Zealand consulate liaison officer, which outlined the deportation process. This ensured they were aware of what to expect upon their return to New Zealand.

Upon arrival, a New Zealand police officer would meet them at the airport.

Emergency housing was available for two days for those whose family or friends were travelling from regional areas to pick them up.

A representative from Centrelink would assist them in filling out forms to apply for payments until they could secure employment.

I had established a rapport with the Consulate Police Liaison Officer, who had been a special guest at a program run by our city's Rotary club for Māori youth—(the eldest sons of their families) participated in the *Standing Tall Leadership Program* facilitated by Dr Ben Pittman.

Recently, during a visit to Australia, New Zealand Prime Minister Jacinda Ardern engaged in discussions with Australian Prime Minister Albanese on various issues, including climate change. She also raised concerns about Australia's deportation policy, advocating for the protection of New Zealand citizens' rights. She acknowledged that those who had committed wrongdoing should be deported but questioned why individuals who had grown up and contributed to Australia were also subject to deportation when New Zealand made different choices regarding Australians living in similar circumstances. Prime

Minister Albanese promised that the immigration department would consider deportation cases on a case-by-case basis with greater sensitivity, marking a potential shift in policy.

Starting from July 1, 2023, the process to become an Australian citizen will be the same for all New Zealand citizens holding an SCV, regardless of when they first arrived in Australia.

Searching for Grace

Reflecting on this particular period in my life, I came to a realisation—I had hitchhiked everywhere, not just locally in New Zealand but also in Australia. It wasn't solely due to a lack of bus fare during my younger days, but rather, it was because I cherished being out on the open road. In a way, I was walking in the footsteps of a pilgrim, traversing the land in search of solace and taking precious moments to contemplate my life. I would pick up and leave repeatedly. I wasn't what people these days might call a "traveller" jetting off overseas for vacations. Instead, I was akin to a meditation practitioner finding tranquility in silence. It was a time when I could focus and hear my inner voice clearly, feeling the earth beneath my feet grounding me. I was on a quest for the wisdom and insight that comes from deep within; I was following my instincts and searching for grace.

Back when I received the diagnosis of Stage 4 cervical cancer, the gynecologist offered me a chance to undergo laser treatment at his day clinic. The urgency was palpable as time was running out, and the procedure had to be done within the week. As I prepared for surgery, I found myself in a quiet waiting room for a brief moment before they called me in for the operation. Another lady who was also waiting sensed my anxiety and asked if I'd like to join her in prayer. Her voice was soothing and calm, reminiscent of my elder sister's, and I felt comforted, knowing I wasn't alone.

When I moved in with my mum, our bond deepened as she opened up about her past. After I got married and had my first child, our relationship evolved, transforming into a genuine friendship as I began to understand her life and our shared experiences. I was in my pre-teens when my mum introduced me to a life philosophy she discovered in Linda Goodman's 1992 book, "Sun Signs". According to this philosophy, my siblings and I were all born two years apart, and our birthdays aligned with specific astrological personality traits. Mum nurtured our strengths and supported our weaknesses, instilling in me the awareness that we all possessed unique gifts. This philosophy piqued my interest in exploring the future through tarot card reading, a passion I shared with my elder sister, who delved deeply into the healing arts.

My mum would regale me with stories of her upbringing by her own grandparents. Her father served as a soldier in the 28th Māori Battalion and tragically lost his life during World War II. His body was laid to rest at the El Alamein Memorial Cemetery in Egypt in 1942. He was on sentry duty, waiting for a relief soldier, but the relieving soldier encountered issues with his weapon. My grandfather valiantly told him to return to camp while he stood guard. Tragically, before the relieved soldier could return, they were ambushed, and my grandfather lost his life. He was posthumously awarded a Medal of Honour, and we commemorate his legacy daily as we cross the Te Hokowhitu Bridge at the entrance to our village in Whakarewarewa, New Zealand. His name is also engraved on the cenotaph at the Auckland Museum.

My mother was a woman of many talents. She was adept at knitting cable jumpers with faux fur and sewing on her Singer sewing machine. She could create trendy outfits and skillfully tackle interior decorating. Our home was adorned with textured and embossed wallpaper, a style you might not find on television but was highly praised by experts on today's lifestyle shows.

Reflecting on our shared experiences, a dear friend recently reminded me of a quote by Baz Luhrmann: "A life lived in fear is a life half-lived". It made me realise that I have conquered all my fears, overcome obstacles, and weathered trials. Documenting these experiences in my book stands as a testament to my strength and resilience.

> *"Grace comes free of charge to people who do not deserve it. I think back to who I was... resentful, wound tight with anger, a single hardened link in a long chain of ungrace learned from family and church. I do so because I know, more surely than I know any pang of healing or forgiveness or goodness I have ever felt, solely comes from the grace of GOD."*
> *(Philip Yancey, 2002)*

(I) Everyone Deserves a Second Chance

During my final days working at Parklea Correctional Centre, I happened upon the surname of a Māori family I knew from New Zealand on the daily muster sheet of inmates housed in units across the prison. An 18-year-old Māori inmate had recently arrived from Surrey Hills Police Station, and his immediate whanau (family) did not reside in Sydney. As I delved into his case notes, I noticed a shift in tone. The custodial staff had discovered him hanging from the ceiling by a rope during a head count, but they managed to reach him in time and cut him down. Medical staff assessed him, and the psychologist was called in to evaluate any injuries that required attention.

I observed that the psychologist had requested the inmate be moved to the clinic and placed in a camera-equipped cell for continuous observation to prevent any further self-harm. A medical regimen was implemented, including wearing a gown, removal of sharp objects, and the use of plastic plates, cups, and cutlery during mealtimes. Clinic custodial staff monitored his behaviour every half-hour for the first day, followed by hourly checks until a further assessment could be made.

I contacted the psychologist to request permission to visit this inmate because I felt genuine sympathy for his situation, given his lack of whanau (family) support in Sydney. The psychologist agreed, and I visited the clinic. There, I asked the custodial officer to unlock the inmate's cell and escort him to the common room for a private conversation. As he walked in with his head down, I noticed fresh rope burns around his throat. I introduced myself and assured him that he was in a safe space. I requested the escort staff return in 20 minutes to provide us with some privacy.

During our conversation, I shared stories about my own background and my grandchildren, trying to establish common ground and put him at ease. I explained that I worked in the prison system and knew about his situation, as well as his lack of family support in Sydney. I reassured him that if he wanted

skills, giving him options for various job prospects upon release. But most importantly, it would allow him to contact his uncle for the family support he sorely needed.

Acknowledgements

I would like to acknowledge the advice and support of my good friend from Scott Westlake Photography for the BIOPIC included in the author's biography. His work can be found via YouTube website: http://www.theholidayhunter.com. Not only his photographic endeavours but his friendship and movie making skills helped me with a compilation video which included excerpts supporting the introduction and anthem to the Pacific Island Offending Program sent to over 20 local magistrates in the South Western region of Sydney.

I would also like to acknowledge the support from members of the public from the Maori and Pacifica community who willingly gave up their time to collaborate in a committee to deliver their expertise and knowledge about integral components within the Pacific Island Offender program. These meetings ran every month for well over a year, and while they unfortunately never eventuated in a start up, they did lead instead to other journeys to support inmates. A special thanks to members such as Malcolm Karipa the Archdeacon of Te Wairua Tapu Church in Sydney, Peter Maa General Manager from Long Bay Correctional Centre, George Clarke (first) Maori Superintendent in NSW and Dr Ben Pittman (deceased) etc.

I would also like to acknowledge the time and effort of my good friend Sally Lim Sun who voluntarily trained six Maori inmates' how to carve bones within a gaol environment over a six week period (the first of its kind in NSW) recognised by TAFE (Technical Adults Further Education) with a statement of attainment, something which enabled them to share time together with the aim of carving an item of cultural significance. The manaias were eventually gifted to the gaol's Cultural Centre and placed in a display cabinet for viewing by staff, other inmates and visitors to Parklea Correctional centre.

Lastly, I would like to acknowledge the work, time and effort of the United church group of volunteers led by Chaplain Liva Tukutama who ran the Student Leadership and Literacy program – a literacy based mentoring program embedding cultural understanding within a student leadership development for Māori and Pacific students.

The workbook was written by the Pacifika community and a copy was provided by Professor Jiorgi Ravulo (Professor and Chair of Social Work Policy studies at the University of Sydney and Adjunct Professor at the University of the South Pacific) as we both participated on the Steering Committee for people of the Pacific for the Attorney Generals department.

References

What's So Amazing About Grace by Philip Yancey (2000), Harper Collins

The Rotorua Second Chance Community – Managed Restorative Justice Programme: An Evaluation by Judi Paulin and Venezia Marlene Kingi, Published Number 36, Dec 2004.

Notes

An Extraordinary Life

Notes

www.ingramcontent.com/pod-product-compliance
Lightning Source LLC
Chambersburg PA
CBHW041146110526
44590CB00027B/4146